Rules of Civility
& Decent Behaviour
In Company and
Converʃation

To My Blessings of Joy, Love,
and Happiness
Carolyn, Jack, and Annie
and Their Mommy and Daddy

Read this together as a family.
I love you!

Also, re-read   Love Abundantly!
at different times   Marmee
living your lives!
                              May 2008

GEORGE WASHINGTON'S

Rules of Civility & Decent Behaviour In Company and Converfation

Introduction by Letitia Baldrige
Annotated by Ann M. Rauscher

The Mount Vernon Ladies' Association
Mount Vernon, Virginia

1 9 8 9

Library of Congress Cataloging-in-Publication Data
Washington, George, 1732-1799.
George Washington's rules of civility & decent behaviour
in company and conversation
I. Etiquette. I. Mount Vernon Ladies' Association
of the Union. II. Title.
E312.78 1989   395'.0973   89-3390
ISBN 0-931917-18-2

Frontispiece: The final major social event in George Washington's life took place on February 22, 1799, when the retired President and General gave away Nelly Custis in marriage at Mount Vernon on his 67th birthday. Miss Custis, Martha Washington's granddaughter, who was raised by the Washington at Mount Vernon, married George Washington's nephew Lawrence Lewis. Washington himself died later that year on the 14th of December, a few weeks after the Lewises' first child was born.

LIST OF ILLUSTRATIONS

PREFACE

When most Americans think of George Washington as a child, they imagine an embarrassed but brave youngster standing with trusty hatchet in hand, next to a fallen cherry tree. "I cannot tell a lie" remains one of Washington's famous quotations, and the cherry tree legend has survived as a testimony to his lifelong honesty.

For more than a century, scholars have been telling us that this brief but memorable episode in Washington's life never really happened. But it is easy to understand why a creative patriot named Parson Mason Weems penned this tale. He must have been unbelievably frustrated to find that we know almost nothing about George Washington's childhood. Parson Weems knew no one would question that the Father of Our Country had confessed to the cherry tree caper, in spite of his young age. Hence, Washington's remarkable reputation has enabled this myth to be passed from generation to generation.

In all likelihood, George Washington's childhood was typical of the period. He played with his brothers and sisters, he learned to ride horses and complete his assigned chores, and he studied his daily lessons with the help of a tutor. Perhaps only one indication of Washington's true potential as a leader, in society as well as in government, stands out to us today. The *Rules of Civility* reflect a youngster's ambition and a boy's determination to become a man. We also see a child's loyalty to the cultural traditions of the mother country.

Those who have studied George Washington's character have often remarked that he followed the *Rules of Civility*, with very few exceptions, until his death in 1799. So, it seems appropriate that the Mount Vernon Ladies' Association, which has devoted its time and resources to the study of George Washington for more than a century, is preserving Washington's guide to good manners. We present them to today's readers just as young George copied them, with the inconsistent grammar, spelling errors and awkward phrasing common in the 18th century.

Fortunately, we have enlisted our nation's "first lady" of good manners to interpret the importance of the *Rules of Civility*. Letitia Baldrige is accustomed to dealing with presidential etiquette, and she is the author of several books devoted to proper behavior in almost every setting, from Parisian parlors to big business boardrooms. She devoted her time, her enthusiasm and her expertise to this project with her trademark sense of style and confidence.

Yet the concept of republishing the *Rules of Civility* in this new and attractive format originated with one of our own Ladies, Mrs. Kenyon C. Bolton, who served the Association with distinction as Vice Regent for Ohio from 1978 to 1988. As chairman of the Publications Committee, she established the highest standards for this unique publication, and her special contributions to the Association assured its financial success.

We are also most grateful to our Vice Regent for Michigan, Mrs. Alexander L. Wiener, who brought this small but special book to fruition, and to Ann Rauscher, who authored the historical annotations.

And once again, we owe our thanks to George Washington himself, who was inspired at the age of 15 to copy these clever and long-lasting epitomes of good manners. Most likely, he would have much preferred to be exploring a nearby forest, learning the ways of a backwoodsman — and perhaps searching for a defenseless cherry tree.

Mrs. Robert Channing Seamans, Jr.
Regent, Mount Vernon Ladies' Association

Rules of Civility & Decent Behaviour In Company and Conversation

1st Every Action done in Company, ought to be with Some Sign of Respect, to those that are Present.

2 When in Company, put not your Hands to any Part of the Body, not usualy Discovered.

3 Shew nothing to your Friend that may affright him.

4 In the Presence of Others Sing not to yourself with a humming Noise, nor Drum with your Fingers or Feet.

5 If You Cough, Sneeze, Sigh, or Yawn, do it not Loud but Privately; and Speak not in your Yawning, but put your handkerchief or Hand before your face and turn aside.

6th Sleep not when others Speak, Sit not when others stand, Speak not when you Should hold your Peace, walk not on when others Stop.

7 Put not off your Cloths in the presence of Others, nor goe out your Chamber half Drest.

8 At Play and at Fire its Good manners to Give Place to the last Commer, and affect not to Speak Louder than Ordinary.

9 Spit not in the Fire, nor Stoop low before it neither Put your Hands into the Flames to warm them, nor Set your Feet upon the Fire specially if there be meat before it.

10 When you Sit down, Keep your Feet firm and Even; without putting one on the other or Crossing them.

11 Shift not yourself in the Sight of others nor Gnaw your nails.

12 Shake not the head, Feet, or Legs rowl not the Eys lift not one eyebrow higher than the other wry not the mouth, and bedew no mans face with your Spittle, by aproaching too near him when you Speak.

INTRODUCTION

*G*eorge Washington wrote his *Rules of Civility &
Decent Behaviour in Company and Conversation* as a
school exercise sometime before he reached the
age of 16. His handwriting on the manuscript is boyish,
his grammar and spelling inferior, but what is of far
greater importance is that this was the code of conduct
that molded his character and helped him assume the
leadership of his country. The importance of this docu-
ment cannot be denied; it influenced our first president
and therefore an entire nation.

The origin of Washington's rules is said to have been
a 17th-century book of etiquette called *Youths Behavior, or
Decency in Conversation Amongst Men,* by Francis Hawkins.
The young Hawkins had, at the age of eight, translated
into English a 16th-century set of behavior rules compiled
by French Jesuits. The code of conduct in Hawkins' book
was simplified and arranged for the schoolboy Washington by an unknown instructor, and the future president
carefully copied the rules into his exercise book, now
preserved at the Library of Congress.

Historians agree that Washington studied Hawkins'
version of the rules and earnestly applied the maxims
throughout his life. What fascinates me, as an observer of

social history, is that the 17th century spawned such a genuine interest in manners, which reached its culmination in the courts of the French King Louis in the 18th century. I find it doubly exciting that George Washington became an 18th-century etiquette writer in his youth, thanks to a French Jesuit treatise that found its way to the New World.

There have been complaints that Washington made no reference to women in his rules, but the entire subject of a gentleman's and a lady's etiquette toward each other was covered in other polished books of the period, mostly published in England. The 15-year-old Washington would certainly have avoided handling such a complicated subject!

Although the young George Washington held the young ladies in the highest regard, particularly one very pretty neighbor named Betsy Fauntleroy, he held no allure for them. The tall, lanky boy, who would later become a very handsome, distinguished adult, was hollow-chested and unprepossessing looking. Yet in his school years, he had already become a leader. One young friend supposedly said of him in his later years, "He was never a prig, had no fights and was often summoned to the playground as a peacemaker, his arbitration in disputes being always accepted."

At the age of 16 Washington was obliged to end his schooling and go to work in order to support his uneducated, widowed mother and his four younger siblings. He must have endured many difficult and melancholic days, but he followed to the fullest the exhortation contained in his own 108th rule: "Honour & Obey your natural parents altho they be Poor." He remained devoted to his mother until she died, "being reverential and gracious to her even when with advancing age she became somewhat morose and exacting while he was loaded with public cares."

In a historical perspective, Washington Irving wrote in 1855 that it was Washington's preoccupation with good behavior at an early age that brought him to the attention of and greatly pleased the powerful, educated family of Lord Fairfax of Virginia. At 17 he was appointed surveyor of the aristocrat's vast estates. As a frequent visitor to Lord Fairfax's "Greenway Court," he learned to comport himself with ease among the rich and titled visitors from England and Europe. It was a totally different milieu from his childhood, one that provided him not only with enjoyment, but also with learning, polish and great political opportunities.

Part of the charm of the adolescent Washington's compilation of his *Rules of Civility* is his tendency to combine several points of social behavior in a single rule. For example, he urges us not to use a foreign tongue around others who do not understand that language, and then in the same sentence says to avoid using vulgar language at any time.

Another part of the charm of his writing is his

sweetness — such as when he exhorts us not to be angry with a business colleague who failed us, because the latter, after all, "tried his best." (Any naiveté in his philosophy may certainly be excused because of a lack of experience at 15!)

Manners and morals were obviously intertwined in George Washington's philosophy, as they should be in any exercise in social behavior. Most of the rules embrace strong moral virtues, which is why it is so interesting to read what he considered to be the most virtuous way of comporting oneself in 18th-century America. The young writer refers constantly to modesty and self restraint; he reminds us of a need for a habitual consideration of others. (These same principles remain today the basis of the philosophy of good manners.) He did, of course, grow up in a much simpler society, in an era in which good and bad behavior were clearly understood by adults. In his time people attended church regularly and discussed the meaning of the sermons with their children. The family was the center of the universe, bound tightly together in order to assure the moral as well as the physical welfare of its members. He would find our society today extremely foreign and probably unkind.

Quite naturally, some of his rules, such as those having to do with gentlemen's boots and the cooking of food on the hearth, no longer apply in today's society. However, most of them, with a slight shift of words, scenes or details, are very relevant to today's problems. What was obviously important to Washington was that the reader understood the bond between good character and a knowledge of social graces. To him the two were one and the same, just as they are to most contemporary writers on manners. He urges us not to spit in public with the same importance that he entreats us not to speak badly of a person who is not present. Both are unkind acts and therefore unacceptable.

The universal appeal of Washington's *Rules of Civility* is evident in the many editions that have been published over the years. The rules were first brought to public attention in 1834 when Jared Sparks selected and edited 57 of the rules to include in the first published edition of Washington's writings. Examples from Washington's code of behavior were published several times, and the rules were mentioned in most of the major 19th-century biographies of Washington. The first complete version of 110 rules appeared in an 1888 publication.

In an 1890 edition published in London, editor Moncure Daniel Conway claimed to be "no fan of Washington," and yet he wrote that "the tone of his character was so entirely that of modesty, he was so fundamentally patriotic, that even his faults transformed to virtues." Conway explained his reason for publishing this project: "These Rules of Civility go forth with the hope they will do more than amuse the reader by their quaintness, and that their story will produce an impression beyond that of its picturesqueness." The

Englishman added, "It is to be hoped that the time is not far distant when in every school right rules of civility will be taught as a main part of the curriculum." It does my heart good to read such a lament made a hundred years ago, because so many of us today are saying the same words and making the same proposal — without much success!

Twentieth-century historians have also been fascinated with the profound influence that Washington's *Rules of Civility* had on his character. John C. Fitzpatrick, who also edited the comprehensive 1932 edition of Washington's writings, commented in his biography of the great man that "many of the Rules of Civility are reflected so clearly in his later life that there is justification for the thought that Washington's youthful training made most lasting impressions upon him." The eminent historian Douglas Southall Freeman, author of the definitive Washington biography, attributed Washington's maturity of character in his early experiences on the frontier to the young man's deliberate decision to adhere to certain moral principles, a code of conduct clearly derived from the *Rules of Civility*.

This 1989 updated edition published for Mount Vernon continues the tradition of examining the early influence of this formal code of conduct on Washington's life. In listing the rules, we have used Washington's own words, with original spelling and punctuation, and have filled in words that had been obliterated in the original manuscript. In addition, we have highlighted some of the rules with examples of their influence on Washington's later experiences. This edition of Washington's rules may be the first in a number of years, but it will undoubtedly not be the last, because historians, sociologists and behaviorists will continue to study the life and works of our first president and dissect his philosophy of manners in terms of their own culture. The valuable lessons contained in the *Rules of Civility* and the insight they provide into Washington's life will not be lost to history.

I hope that both children and adults will enjoy this little book, and ponder what the Father of Our Country felt was so important when he was a young boy. Not all of the rules will be meaningful to the reader, but one cannot sit peacefully reading them without being touched. What leaves me in absolute awe is the brilliance and initiative the young Washington demonstrated in spending the time and the care on a subject that is generally so far removed from an adolescent's priorities. As he matured and rose in prominence, he obviously attempted to practice what he preached, and set a lasting example in moral leadership for us to admire. If a young American is looking for a role model, he or she need look no farther than Mount Vernon, Virginia, and a study of the life and times of the man who lived there.

Letitia Baldrige

Rules of Civility & Decent Behaviour In Company and Converſation

1st Every Action done in Company, ought to be with Some Sign of Respect, to those that are Present.

Even when he was the highest-ranking official, Washington never failed to be respectful and courteous to those around him. A Frenchman who met the General during the Revolutionary War remarked, "I have never seen anyone who was more naturally and spontaneously polite." Another admirer of Washington said that "his manners are those of one perfectly accustomed to society, quite a rare thing in America."

Rule Number 26: "In Pulling off your Hat to Persons of Distinction, as Noblemen, Justices, Churchmen &c make a Reverence, bowing more or less according to the Custom of the Better Bred, and Quality of the Person." Martha Washington's weekly "levees" during the presidency provided the occasion for the ladies and gentlemen of society to pay their respects to the first lady. The President himself joined his wife at many of these receptions and greeted guests according to the proper customs of the day.

2^d When in Company, put not your Hands to any Part of the Body, not usually Discovered.

3^d Shew Nothing to your Friend that may affright him.

4 In the Presence of Others Sing not to yourself with a humming Noise, nor Drum with your Fingers or Feet.

5th: If You Cough, Sneeze, Sigh, or Yawn, do it not Loud but Privately; and Speak not in your Yawning, but put Your handkercheif or Hand before your face and turn aside.

6th Sleep not when others Speak, Sit not when others stand, Speak not when you Should hold your Peace, walk not on when others Stop.

7th: Put not off your Cloths in the presence of Others, nor go out your Chamber half Drest

8th: At Play and at Fire its Good manners to Give Place to the last Commer, and affect not to Speak Louder than Ordinary

9th: Spit not in the Fire, nor Stoop low before it neither Put your Hands into the Flames to warm them, nor Set your Feet upon the Fire especially if there be meat before it

When you Sit down, Keep your Feet firm and Even, without putting one on the other or Crossing them

11th: Shift not yourself in Sight of others nor Gnaw your nails

12th: Shake not the head, Feet, or Legs rowl not the Eys lift not one eyebrow higher than the other wry not the mouth, and bedew no mans face with your Spittle, by approaching too near him when you Speak

13th: Kill no Vermin as Fleas, lice ticks &c in the Sight of Others, if you See any filth or thick Spittle put your foot Dexteriously upon it if it be upon the Cloths of your Companions, Put it off privately, and if it be upon your own Cloths return Thanks to him who puts it off

14th: Turn not your Back to others especially in Speaking, Jog not the Table or Desk on which Another reads or writes, lean not upon any one

15th Keep your Nails clean and Short, also your Hands and Teeth Clean, yet without Shewing any great Concern for them

A rule of etiquette mentioning teeth brings to mind Washington's infamous dental problems. Although he never possessed wooden teeth, he wore a full set of dentures made from ivory and cow's teeth by the time he was 58. Washington certainly would have considered the state of his teeth to be an unfit subject for polite discussion, being careful not to publicly show "any great Concern" for such a personal matter. In private, Washington sought help from his dentist, who advised his client that cleaning the dentures "with brush and some Chalk scraped fine" would whiten the teeth and improve their appearance. Washington's efforts to conceal his dental problems were not always successful, and the President was greatly distressed when an ill-fitting set of false teeth distorted the appearance of his mouth. The result can be seen in the tight-lipped expression on Washington's face in Gilbert Stuart's famous 1796 portrait, for which Washington posed while wearing a particularly uncomfortable set of dentures that he soon replaced.

16th Do not Puff up the Cheeks, Loll not out the tongue rub the hands or beard, thrust out the lips, or bite them or keep the Lips too open or too Close

17th Be no Flatterer, neither Play with any that delights not to be Play'd Withal.

Read no Letters, Books or Papers in Company when there is a Necessity for the doing of it you must ask leave: come not near the Books or Writings of Another so as to read them unless desired or give your opinion of them unask'd also look not nigh when another is writing a Letter.

Washington considered his study at Mount Vernon to be his private sanctum, where away from company he could retire to read or write. Despite the large number of guests at Mount Vernon, Washington sought the solitude of the room containing his library to work on correspondence, away from guests as proper etiquette demanded. Washington's daily routine began and ended in his study. An early riser, Washington worked in his study several hours from before sunrise until breakfast was served at 7:00 a.m. After a busy day, he still found time to read or write for at least another hour before retiring at night.

19![th] let your Countenance be pleasant but in Serious Matters Somewhat grave.

20![th] The Gestures of the Body must be Suited to the discourse you are upon.

Washington realized the importance of suiting his gestures and demeanor to his demanding role as commander in chief of the Continental Army during the war. Called a "born leader," the General was described as "tall, his face was commanding, his eyes were kind, his gestures and words simple; and above all a calm and firm behaviour harmonized all these qualities." At nearly 6'3" tall, Washington certainly presented an impressive and commanding figure, which no doubt enhanced his already inspiring appearance.

Rule Number 19: "let your Countenance be pleasant but in Serious Matters Somewhat grave." Although marriage is indeed a serious matter, George Washington's wedding to Martha Custis on January 6, 1759 must have filled him with happiness. The grave expression on his face is suitable to the dignity of the ceremony, but was no doubt replaced by a pleasant countenance at the conclusion of the event that marked the beginning of a long and enduring marriage, which lasted until his death in 1799.

21st Reproach none for the Infirmities of Nature, nor Delight to Put them that have in mind thereof.

22^{d} Shew not yourself glad at the Misfortune of another though he were your enemy.

23^{d} When you see a Crime punished, you may be inwardly Pleased; but always shew Pity to the Suffering Offender.

24th Do not laugh too loud or too much at any Publick Spectacle.

25th Superfluous Complements and all Affectation of Ceremonie are to be avoided, yet where due they are not to be Neglected

26th In Pulling off your Hat to Persons of Distinction, as Noblemen, Justices, Churchmen &c make a Reverence, bowing more or less according to the Custom of the Better Bred, and Quality of the Person. Amongst your equals expect not always that they Should begin with you first, but to Pull off the Hat when there is no need is Affectation, in the Manner of Saluting and resaluting in words keep to the most usual Custom

27th. Tis ill manners to bid one more eminent than yourself be covered as well as not to do it to whom it's due Likewise he that makes too much haste to Put on his hat does not well, yet he ought to Put it on at the first, or at most the Second time of being ask'd; now what is herein Spoken, of Qualification in behaviour in Saluting, ought also to be observed in taking of Place, and Sitting down for ceremonies without Bounds is troublesome

28th. If any one come to Speak to you while you are Sitting Stand up tho he be your Inferior, and when you Present Seats let it be to every one according to his Degree

29th. When you meet with one of Greater Quality than yourself, Stop, and retire especially if it be at a Door or any Straight place to give way for him to Pass

30th. In walking the highest Place in most Countrys seems to be on the right hand therefore Place yourself on the left of him whom you desire to Honour: but if three walk together the middest Place is the most Honourable the wall is usually given to the most worthy if two walk together

Rule Number 32: "To one that is your equal, or not much inferior you are to give the cheif Place in your Lodging. . . ." Among the many distinguished men of the late 18th century to visit Mount Vernon was Jacques Pierre Brissot de Warville, a well-known French journalist. Brissot received the famous Mount Vernon hospitality during a trip through America in 1788, while he was working on a history of the new nation. Hundreds of travelers, both famous and common, were offered lodging at Mount Vernon, prompting Washington to refer to his home as "a well resorted tavern" from which few were ever turned away.

31st If anyone far Surpasses others, either in age, Estate, or Merit, yet would give Place to a meaner than himself in his own lodging or elsewhere the one ought not to except it, So he on the other part should not use much earnestness nor offer it above once or twice.

32^{d} To one that is your equal, or not much inferior you are to give the cheif Place in your Lodging and he to who 'tis offered ought at the first to refuse it but at the Second to accept though not without acknowledging his own unworthiness.

The hospitality of Mount Vernon was known far and wide. Visitors were accommodated in one of the seven guest bedchambers in the Mansion, including the "Lafayette room" where the illustrious Frenchman stayed during his 1784 visit. A popular host, Washington once compared his home to "a well resorted tavern, as scarcely any strangers who are going from north to south, or from south to north, do not spend a day or two at it." In his diary for 1785, Washington recorded an incredible 423 visitors for the year. The frequency and number of guests prompted Washington to note an unusual occurrence in 1797, when he and Mrs. Washington dined alone for the first time in 20 years.

33^{d} They that are in Dignity or in office have in all places Preceedency but whilst they are Young they ought to respect those that are their equals in Birth or other Qualitys, though they have no Publick charge.

34th It is good Manners to prefer them to whom we Speak before ourselves, especially if they be above us with whom in no Sort we ought to begin.

35th Let your Discourse with Men of Business be Short and Comprehensive.

Rule Number 35: "Let your Discourse with Men of Business be Short and Comprehensive." In 1753, at the age of 21, Washington was entrusted with an important mission by Lieutenant Governor Dinwiddie of Virginia, who sent the young man into the Ohio territory to deliver an ultimatum to the French forces stationed there. Washington's entry into the world of military diplomacy proved to be an eventful beginning to a long, turbulent and ultimately successful military career.

36th Artificers & Persons of low Degree ought not to use many ceremonies to Lords, or Others of high Degree but Respect and highly Honour them, and those of high Degree ought to treat them with affibility and Courtesie, without Arrogancy

Washington's views regarding "ceremonies to Lords" helped to determine many of the customs associated with the office of President which still survive today. Although courtesy to persons "of high Degree" was always considered a sign of respect, Washington felt that the President should not be equated with royalty. As the official form of address, he preferred "Mr. President" to "His Highness, the President of the United States of America, and Protector of their Liberties," the elaborate and cumbersome title favored by the Senate.

37th In Speaking to men of Quality do not lean nor Look them full in the Face, nor approach too near them at lest Keep a full Pace from them

38th: In visiting the Sick, do not Presently play the Physicion if you be not Knowing therein

Rule Number 41: "Undertake not to Teach your equal in the art himself Proffesses. . . ." Washington's early career as a surveyor provided an invaluable learning experience for the young man. A quick learner, the eager teenager soon became quite proficient in the art of surveying. Nonetheless, he continued to show respectful deference to his equals and superiors in the field, including the influential Fairfax family, who gave him his first job as a surveyor.

Rule Number 42: "*Let thy ceremonies in Courtesie be proper to the Dignity of his place with whom thou conversest. . . .*" *One of the most moving moments in Washington's career came on December 4, 1783, when he bade farewell to his Revolutionary War officers at Fraunces Tavern in New York. With tears in his eyes, the General embraced each of the men, and with dignity and grace, turned and left the room to begin his journey to Annapolis to resign his commission and head home to Mount Vernon.*

39th In writing or Speaking, give to every Person his due Title According to his Degree & the Custom of the Place.

40th Strive not with your Superiers in argument, but always Submit your Judgment to others with Modesty

41st Undertake not to Teach your equal in the art himself Proffesses; it Savours of arrogancy

42nd Let thy ceremonies in Courtesie be proper to the Dignity of his place with whom thou conversest for it is absurd to act ye same with a Clown and a Prince

For the official ceremonies during the presidency, Washington was determined to avoid the trappings of royalty. Rather than imposing majestic behavior on guests, the President and his wife greeted citizens with courteous refinement. Abigail Adams, in describing a reception, favorably compared Washington to the British monarch, observing that the President greeted his guests "with a grace, dignity and ease, that leaves Royal George far behind him."

Rule Number 46: "Take all Admonitions thankfully in what Time or Place Soever given. . . ." The story of young George Washington chopping down a cherry tree is only a legend, but the popular myth reflects the image of a respectful, honest child. Many stories about Washington that appeared after his death reinforced his reputation as an honest, good man whose code of conduct should be admired and followed by all Americans.

43^{d} Do not express Joy before one sick or in pain for that contrary Passion will aggravate his Misery.

44th When a man does all he can though it Succeeds not well blame not him that did it.

45th Being to advise or reprehend any one, consider whether it ought to be in publick or in Private; presently, or at Some other time in what terms to do it & in reproving Shew no Sign of Cholar but do it with all Sweetness and Mildness

46th Take all Admonitions thankfully in what Time or Place Soever given but afterwards not being culpable take a Time & Place convenient to let him know it that gave them.

47th: Mock not nor Jest at anything of Importance break no Jest that are Sharp Biting, and if you Deliver any thing witty and Pleasent abstain from Laughing thereat yourself.

Although Washington's popular image is one of reserved dignity, he was not without a sense of humor. A visitor to Mount Vernon recalled, "He appeared to enjoy a humorous observation and made several himself. He laughed heartily sometimes and in a very good humored manner." Clearly capable of delivering "witty and Pleasent" observations, Washington exhibited this side of his personality only to close friends and family. His nephew Howell Lewis noted that "when in a lively mood" his uncle was "so full of pleasantry, so agreeable to all with whom he associated, that I could hardly realize that he was the same Washington whose dignity awed all who approached him."

48th: Wherein you reprove Another be unblameable yourself; for example is more prevalent than Precepts

49 Use no Reproachfull Language against any one neither Curse nor Revile

50th: Be not hasty to beleive flying Reports to the Disparagement of any

51st Wear not your Cloths, foul, unript or Dusty but See they be Brush'd once every day at least and take heed that you approach not to any uncleaness

52^{d} In your Apparel be Modest and endeavor to accomodate Nature, rather than to procure Admiration keep to the Fashion of your equals Such as are Civil and orderly with respect to Times and Places

A fine example of Washington suiting his apparel to the time and place occurred at his first inauguration in 1789. To promote American industry, Washington wore a specially-made suit of brown broadcloth manufactured in Hartford, Connecticut, rather than a fashionable European import. The finishing touch on the outfit was a set of brass buttons picturing an American eagle.

53^{d} Run not in the Streets, neither go too slowly nor with Mouth open go not Shaking y^{r} Arms kick not the earth with y^{r} feet, go not upon the Toes, nor in a Dancing fashion.

54th: Play not the Peacock, looking every where about you, to See if you be well Deck't, if your Shoes fit well if your Stockings Sit neatly, and Cloths handsomely.

Washington was determined to instill the code of conduct contained in his Rules of Civility into the minds of the next generation. To his nephew Bushrod Washington he wrote, "Do not conceive that fine Clothes make fine Men, any more than fine feathers make fine Birds. A plain genteel dress is more admired and obtains more credit than lace and embroidery in the Eyes of the judicious and sensible."

55th: Eat not in the Streets, nor in ye House, out of Season

56th: Associate yourself with Men of good Quality if you Esteem your own Reputation; for 'tis better to be alone than in bad Company

As a young man, Washington constantly strove to better himself, and his early association with the prestigious Fairfax family was crucial to the development of his character. Through William Fairfax, a Mount Vernon neighbor whose daughter married George's older half brother, Washington was introduced to the world of aristocracy for which his training in proper etiquette had prepared him. Fairfax gave Washington his first job as a surveyor and started Washington on the path to greatness.

Rule Number 56: "Associate yourself with Men of good Quality if you Esteem your own Reputation; for 'tis better to be alone than in bad Company." Throughout his life Washington surrounded himself with men of good quality, from his early associations with the prominent Fairfax family to his esteemed colleagues during the Revolutionary War and the presidency. Here, Washington plays host at Mount Vernon to the Marquis de Lafayette, who served under the General during the American Revolution and went on to greater glory in his native country during the French Revolution.

57th: In walking up and Down in a House, only with One in Company if he be Greater than yourself, at the first give him the Right hand and Stop not till he does, and be not the first that turns, and when you do turn let it be with your face towards him, if he be a Man of Great Quality, walk not with him Cheek by Joul but Somewhat behind him; but yet in Such a Manner that he may easily Speak to you

58th: Let your Conversation be without Malice or Envy, for 'tis a Sign of a Tractable and Commendable Nature: And in all Causes of Passion admit Reason to Govern

59th: Never express anything unbecoming, nor Act agst ye Rules Moral before your inferiours

60th Be not immodest in urging your Friends to Discover a Secret

61st Utter not base and frivilous things amongst grave and Learn'd Men nor very Difficult Questians or Subjects, among the Ignorant or things hard to be believed, Stuff not your Discourse with Sentences amongst your Betters nor Equals

62^{d} Speak not of doleful Things in a Time of Mirth or at the Table; Speak not of Melancholy Things as Death and Wounds, and if others Mention them Change if you can the Discourse tell not your Dreams, but to your intimate Friend

63.^{d} A Man ought not to value himself of his Atchievements, or rare Qualities of wit; much less of his riches Virtue or Kindred

64th Break not a Jest where none takes pleasure in mirth Laugh not aloud, nor at all without Occasion, deride no mans Misfortune, tho' there seem to be Some cause

Although Washington was not one to laugh "without Occasion," he certainly was not entirely deprived of entertainment. He frequently attended the theatre and found there an appropriate outlet for laughter. A friend observed in 1787, "His air was serious and reflecting, yet I have seen him in theatre laughing heartily." What a refreshing thought to imagine Washington enjoying a play!

Rule Number 69: "If two contend together take not the part of either unconstrained. . . ." The future peacemaker intervenes in a schoolboy fight in this 19th-century engraving of a fictitious event in Washington's childhood. Even though he was in his early teens when he copied the Rules of Civility, it is pleasing to think that he followed a code of proper behavior from an early age.

65th Speak not injurious Words neither in Jest nor Earnest Scoff at none although they give Occasion

66th Be not froward but friendly and Courteous; the first to Salute hear and answer & be not Pensive when it's a time to Converse

67th Detract not from others neither be excessive in Commanding

68th Go not thither, where you know not, whether you Shall be Welcome or not. Give not Advice whth being Ask'd & when desired do it briefly

69 If two contend together take not the part of either unconstrained; and be not obstinate in your own Opinion, in Things indiferent be of the Major Side

70th Reprehend not the imperfections of others for that belongs to Parents Masters and Superiours

71st Gaze not on the marks or blemishes of Others and ask not how they came. What you may Speak in Secret to your Friend deliver not before others

72^{d} Speak not in an unknown Tongue in Company but in your own Language and that as those of Quality do and not as ye Vulgar; Sublime matters treat Seriously

Rule Number 71: ". . . What you may Speak in Secret to your Friend deliver not before others." Although the words exchanged during George and Martha Washington's first meeting are forever lost to history, it is evident that theirs was a supportive and loving relationship that transcended time and distance. Of the numerous letters exchanged throughout their 45-year marriage, however, only two survive. Aware that future generations would be privy to their personal correspondence, Martha Washington chose to burn all the letters between herself and her husband, and only the two letters that managed to escape the inferno remain as a testament to their enduring relationship.

73^{d} Think before you Speak pronounce not imperfectly nor bring out your Words too hastily but orderly & distinctly

A thoughtful and careful speaker, Washington mastered the delicate art of conversation early and drew admiration from associates for his controlled manner of speaking: "In conversation he looks you full in the face, is deliberate, definitive and engaging. His voice is agreeable rather than strong. His demeanor at all times composed and dignified." Washington was also hailed for his public speeches, not because of outstanding oratorical skills, but for the simplicity and sincerity of his delivery. His first inaugural address in 1789, it was said, brought tears to the eyes of listeners, confirming the entrancing spell of their leader's inspiring speaking ability.

74th: When Another Speaks be attentive your Self and disturb not the Audience if any hesitate in his Words help him not nor Prompt him without desired, Interrupt him not, nor Answer him till his Speech be ended

75th In the midst of Discourse ask not of what one treateth but if you Perceive any Stop because of your coming you may well intreat him gently to Proceed: If a Person of Quality comes in while your Conversing it's handsome to Repeat what was said before

76th While you are talking, Point not with your Finger at him of Whom you Discourse nor Approach too near him to whom you talk especially to his face

77th Treat with men at fit Times about Business & Whisper not in the Company of Others

78th Make no Comparisons and if any of the Company be Commended for any brave act of Vertue, commend not another for the Same

79th Be not apt to relate News if you know not the truth thereof. In Discoursing of things you Have heard Name not your Author always A Secret Discover not

80th Be not Tedious in Discourse or in reading unless you find the Company pleased therewith

81st Be not Curious to Know the Affairs of Others neither approach those that Speak in Private

82^{d} Undertake not what you cannot Perform but be Carefull to keep your Promise

On two momentous occasions in his life, Washington took on enormous responsibilities in the service of his country: as commander in chief of the Continental Army and as first President of the United States. As he accepted the former, he modestly told the Congress that "I do not think myself equal to the command I am honored with," yet vowed to "exert every power I possess in their service, and for the support of the glorious cause."

83^{d} When you deliver a matter do it without Passion & with Discretion, however mean ye Person be you do it too

84th. When your Superiours talk to any Body, hearken not, neither Speak nor Laugh

85th: In Company of these of Higher Quality than yourself Speak not till you are ask'd a Question then Stand upright put of your Hat & Answer in few words

86 In Disputes, be not So Desireous to Overcome as not to give Liberty to each one to deliver his Opinion and Submit to ye Judgment of ye Major Part especially if they are Judges of the Dispute

87th Let thy carriage be such as becomes a Man Grave Settled and attentive to that which is spoken. Contradict not at every turn what others Say

Washington consistently impressed those who encountered him with his strong, dignified manner. During the war, a Frenchman described his first impression of the man: "I could not keep my eyes from that imposing countenance; grave, yet not severe; affable, without familiarity. Its predominant expression was calm dignity."

88th: Be not tedious in Discourse, make not many Digressions, nor repeat often the Same manner of Discourse

89th Speak not Evil of the absent for it is unjust

90 Being Set at meat Scratch not neither Spit Cough or blow your Nose except there's a Necessity for it

91st Make no Shew of taking great Delight in your Victuals, Feed not with Greediness; cut your Bread with a Knife, lean not on the Table, neither find fault with what you Eat

92 Take no Salt or cut Bread with your Knife Greasy

Rule Number 93: "Entertaining any one at table it is decent to present him w.^{t} meat. . . ." Visitors to Mount Vernon often commented on the gracious hospitality and bountiful table at the Washington home. According to Martha Washington's grandson George Washington Parke Custis, one of his grandmother's home-cured hams was boiled at Mount Vernon every day. A typical dinner featured several kinds of meat, and cold meat was served for breakfast.

93 Entertaining any one at table it is decent to present him w! meat, Undertake not to help others undesired by y^e Master

The Washingtons offered their dinner guests at Mount Vernon a hearty feast. Dinner, served at three in the afternoon, was a multicourse banquet featuring soup, a variety of meats, fish and vegetables, a tempting assortment of desserts, and several fine wines. A visitor in 1799 described a meal consisting of "leg of boiled beef, mutton chops, hommony, cabbage, potatoes, pickles, fried tripe, onions, . . . mince pies, tarts, cheese . . . nuts, apples, raisins." Depending on the number of guests, dinner was served in either the smaller family dining room or the large banquet hall added to the Mansion in 1776. One guest reported that Martha Washington presided at the head of the table, with her husband seated to her right. The warm and gracious Mount Vernon hospitality made dining with the Washingtons an unforgettable experience.

94th If you Soak bread in the Sauce let it be no more than what you put in your Mouth at a time and blow not your broth at Table but Stay till Cools of it Self

95th Put not your meat to your Mouth with your Knife in your hand neither Spit forth the Stones of any fruit Pye upon a Dish nor Cast anything under the table

96 It's unbecoming to Stoop much to ones Meat Keep your Fingers clean & when foul wipe them on a Corner of your Table Napkin

97th Put not another bit into your Mouth til the former be Swallowed let not your Morsels be too big for the Gowls.

98th Drink not nor talk with your mouth full neither Gaze about you while you are a Drinking

99th Drink not too leisurely nor yet too hastily. Before and after Drinking wipe your Lips breath not then or Ever with too great a Noise, for its uncivil

Washington was fond of wine and offered his dinner guests at Mount Vernon both port and Madeira. The latter seems to have been Washington's favorite drink, judging from his frequent orders for huge quantities of the "choicest Madeira wine." A visitor in 1798 reported that Washington "loves to chat after dinner with a glass of Madeira in his hand," and Martha's granddaughter Nelly Custis wrote that Washington typically enjoyed three glasses of Madeira in the evening. A dinner guest fondly recalled the end of one memorable meal at Mount Vernon, when Washington raised his glass and toasted "All our Friends."

100 Cleanse not your teeth with the Table Cloth Napkin Fork or Knife but if Others do it let it be done w! a Pick Tooth

101st Rince not your Mouth in the Presence of Others

102^d It is out of use to call upon the Company often to Eat nor need you Drink to others every Time you Drink

103^d In Company of your Betters be not longer in eating than they are lay not your Arm but only your hand upon the table

104th It belongs to y^e. Chiefest in Company to unfold his Napkin and fall to Meat first, But he ought then to Begin in time & to Dispatch with Dexterity that ye Slowest may have time allowed him

105th. Be not Angry at Table whatever happens & if you have reason to be so, shew it not but on a Cheerfull Countenance especially if there be Strangers for Good Humour makes one Dish of Meat a Feast

Though good manners prevented Washington from commenting on it at the time, he recorded in his diary with great amusement the refreshments offered at a ball he attended in Alexandria: "plenty of Bread and Butter, some Biscuits with Tea, and Coffee which the Drinkers of could not Distinguish from Hot water sweetened." The service apparently was also lacking, for Washington noted "that pocket handkerchiefs servd the purposes of Table Cloths & Napkins and that no Apologies were made for either." Washington dubbed the meager banquet that evening the "Bread and Butter Ball."

106th Set not yourself at y^e upper of y^e Table but if it be your Due or that y^e Master of y^e house will have it So, Contend not, least you Should Trouble y^e Company

Rule Number 109: "Let your Recreations be Manfull not Sinfull." The amusements and recreations offered to guests at Mount Vernon reflected the gracious manner of the master of the estate. Whether strolling through the pleasure garden or bowling on the green, visitors to Washington's home were made welcome by the family and often were encouraged to stay as long as they pleased.

107th. If others talk at Table be attentive but talk not with Meat in your Mouth

108th. When you Speak of God or His Attributes, let it be Seriously & with Reverence. Honour & Obey your Natural Parents altho they be Poor

Washington's father died when young George was only 11, leaving the boy to care for his widowed mother and four younger siblings. Washington's older brothers from his father's first marriage inherited the finer properties, while Mary Ball Washington and her young family had to survive on a lesser inheritance. Washington continued to help support his mother throughout her long life, visiting her for the last time just before his first inauguration in 1789. She died a few months later, knowing that her eldest son was President of the United States.

109th. Let your Recreations be Manfull not Sinfull.

110th. Labour to keep alive in your Breast that Little Spark of Celestial fire Called Conscience.

F I N I S

The text of this edition of George Washington's Rules of Civility & Decent Behaviour *has been set in the 1968 version of Merganthaler VIP New Baskerville. This type preserves the original italic swash caps designed in 1757 by the English printer and publisher John Baskerville. A native of rural Worcestershire, Baskerville was an innovator whose designs represent the epitome of the Transitional Style which bridged Old Style and Modern typography. The display types are set in Fry's Baskerville by Isaac Moore, 1768, and Snell Roundhand Script by Matthew Carter, 1965 (patterned after Charles Snell, 1694). The book was composed by General Typographers, Inc., of Washington, D.C., and printed by Wolk Press of Woodlawn, Maryland. The paper is 100 pound Mohawk Superfine text, an acid-free sheet manufactured by Mohawk Paper Mills, Inc., of Cohoes, New York. The design is by Robert Wiser and Marc Alain Meadows of Meadows & Wiser, Washington, D.C.*